# Charisma

## *EXPRESS*

Charisma Express

# Charisma

## *EXPRESS*

Know How to Be Charismatic

**Brandon Bryce & KnowIt Express**

N2K Publication

ISBN 978-1-533-05214-8

Printed in the United States of America

First Edition

Welcome to the *Know It Express* - the express lane to knowledge!

To stay up-to-date, please be sure to sign up for **our newsletter** at http://www.KnowItExpress.com and follow us on social media:

https://www.facebook.com/KnowItExpress
https://twitter.com/KnowItExpress
https://plus.google.com/+KnowItExpress

Charisma Express

# EXPRESS LANE

Charisma Express

*CHAPTER 1*

# Attract Magnetic Power as a Charismatic Person

### The X-Factor

We all know a person so charming, so magnanimous, and so influential that everyone is drawn to them. We bask in their presence, vie for their attention, and try to emulate them.

You know who we're talking about...the **charismatic genius** who always knows what to say and how to act, and when they speak, everyone listens thinking *"Wow! I can't help but agree with everything they say!"*

Even though deep down inside we'd all like to be treated like them, people with the kind of charisma needed to stand out and be recognized are rare in this world.

When other people don't recognize that quality within us, we may resign ourselves to being or believing that we're boring, powerless nobodies; however, charisma does not need to be exclusive to certain people.

## What Is Charisma?

Charisma can be defined as "a compelling appeal or charm that can inspire the attraction of others" or "a personal magic of leadership arousing popular enthusiasm."

One fictional character that fits this description is **Jay Gatsby** from the legendary American writer F. Scott Fitzgerald's greatest work <u>The Great Gatsby</u>. He exudes an aura of stylish coolness and enigma, which outsiders can't help but be drawn to.

Now of course you don't need to hide in an ivory tower and only emerge when necessary in order to stay mysterious. Nor do you need to know how to make a stylish grand entrance that makes people wonder "Who is this person?"

Some of the most charismatic people have been world leaders from Ronald Reagan, Nelson Mandela, and Mahatma Gandhi to businessmen like Richard Branson and media personalities like Oprah Winfrey.

## The Charismatic Edge

There is no doubt that charismatic people are fascinating individuals. They inspire us and understand something we don't: **charisma is power.**

- <u>Relationships</u>: Charismatic people don't hesitate to draw others into conversations. When you are charismatic, you will be able to take the initiative to reach out instead of watching the world from the sidelines. If you are shy or lack confidence, this will make an especially huge difference to you.

- <u>Popularity</u>: As you begin to inspire people, they will join you. For the uncharismatic, it is more comfortable to flock to a leader than to go rogue. You might be surprised to learn just how few people are comfortable in their skin. These are the people who will support you enthusiastically.

- <u>Presence</u>: As a charismatic person, you will begin to feel more positively about yourself and what you believe in. This positivity will make you feel comfortable in your body and in the world around you. This kind of comfort translates into better presence. The way you carry yourself through the world shows a lot about your own confidence and positivity.

- <u>Attractiveness</u>: We are naturally attracted to charismatic people because they are not a dime a dozen, but a needle in a haystack with desirable qualities very few have and that are difficult to maintain.

Charismatic people experience some of these benefits and many more as a part of their daily lives...just like you will as soon you learn to be charismatic too!

As a note, this is not going to be the study of charismatic people of the past, but rather a hands-on application-based study covering key elements about yourself you can harness to become more charismatic.

## CHAPTER 2

# Make Wise Decision as a Charismatic Person

### The End Vision

We are inspired by those who set a goal and overcome all odds to attain it.

Unfortunately, many of us are preoccupied with feelings that weaken our resolve or prevent us from attaining our goals. If you are too busy nursing hurt feelings to achieve awe-inspiring feats, you will lose all popular support.

This leads us to the <u>first important quality</u> that all charismatic people have: **focus**.

Naturally-born leaders attract people to them effortlessly by inspiring them. They tend to focus on their goals and not on their setbacks or details that only steer them off course. They are not sidetracked by the goals of other people, or by naysayers, or distracting emotions.

Charismatic people can abstract diminishing emotions such as jealousy, mockery, or anger and project a pervasively **neutral attitude**. A neutral attitude makes you appear even-keeled and trustworthy. Charismatic people, especially those in the public eye like politicians or journalists, remain unfazed by attackers by staying focused.

## The Neutrality Lure

What we are going to discus next is the "**Neutrality Lure**" (or **Neutralurety**). It involves training your brain to handle situation in a certain way effectively. It is so named because you use a gesture to "lure" your brain out of an *emotional reaction* and into **calm neutrality.**

> Example: Imagine that you are confronted by a bunch of people teasing someone. They invite you to join their childish enterprise. You have better things to do than make fun of people, but in the heat of the moment you might be tongue-tied. So how can you reason with these people?

The "Neutrality Lure" will help you say the exact right thing. First adopt the body language that will trigger your charismatic behavior.

> 1. Stance: Adopting the right stance and gesture is crucial. When the need arises, you will lower your arms in front of your belly and cross your hands.

> 2. Signal: Mentally register what this stance means. In a matter of seconds you are sending a message to your brain to focus on a neutral attitude.

3. <u>Speak</u>: As soon as the signal is sent, your brain will respond with a mature, wise, and charismatic reaction.

Explanation:

Now what is it about this stance and gesture that makes you able to respond neutrally?

When you cross your hands in front of your belly, your mind will calm and center. It will give you the space to think and to speak wisely and neutrally. You might say, "Sorry, I cannot be a part of this" or "I wouldn't know how to make fun of a stranger." and be on your way.

## Guiding Response Through Body Gesture

Let's look at why you need to send a message to your brain when confronted with stressful situations. The answer is simply that most of the time we don't know how to react.

Social situations involving confrontation or awkwardness create a *"fight or flight"* reaction. Physiologically, this means an increased heart-rate and a diversion of blood away from the brain leaving us physically incapable of producing a proper response.

By **physically** adopting a neutral body stance first will allow you to produce a proper response with a neutral mind. Think of this as if you were having a bad day and you were to physically force a smile onto your face. A happy mood would follow suit via *leading with your body*.

Research shows that stance and gesture affect the brain through muscle memory.

This particular signal, your hands crossed in front of your belly, is a calm, non-confrontational position that triggers a **neutral reaction**. It will remind you to stay focused on your purpose and will instantly dispel the "flight or fight" reaction.

Example: Imagine you are brought in to play the mediator between two friends arguing about a money issue. This is a good example because it can be difficult to stay unbiased with friends. Frequently we want to support one friend's case over another's because we like them more, relate to their situation more, or a hundred other reasons. How do you handle that situation with charisma? The best way to avoid conflict is to remain unbiased. So stand, signal, and speak:

1. Stand: put your hands together in front of your belly,
2. Signal: send the neutrality signal to your brain, and
3. Speak: calmly think of a solution that will help both of your friends equally.

Your friends will be grateful for a solution that solves the problem fairly, even if it doesn't make everybody happy.

The more you practice that neutral attitude, the more you will gain respect and grow your reputation as a charismatic person. Just try to use the Neutralurety inconspicuously.

## <u>Exercise</u>: Center Yourself

Stand in front of a mirror and train your brain by imagining what you would say or do with the following exercises. Practice Stand, Signal, Speak and focus on a calm, neutral response.

If you finish these exercises, think of a few of your own scenarios. There's no such thing as too much practice.

1.) You are about to give a speech and the audience is making too much noise.

2.) You are faced with a noisy and threatening driver who just bumped into your car.

3.) You are negotiating a deal with business people from overseas and a different culture.

Remember to adopt the right body language before you act. Learn to lure your brain by crossing your hands in front of your belly. After you do it a few times it will become an instinct and you will be able to remain calm and neutral in even the most uncomfortable confrontations.

*CHAPTER 3*

# Establish Powerful Presence Anywhere as a Charismatic Person

## Positivity Is The Absence Of Negativity

Now that you know how to gain some charisma with focus, let's work on **presence**.

Presence is "a noteworthy quality of poise and effectiveness" or "the impressive manner or appearance of a person." All to say it's the impact you have on people when you interact with them, which you want to do positively.

To have a memorable presence, you must be able to isolate and reject negative feedback and ignore the emotions that make you vulnerable and hold you back. Being positive is mostly about diverting negativity.

Paying attention to what people say around you, whether they are whispering or spreading rumors, can trigger emotions like anger, doubt, or anxiety that can cause you to lose the courage to speak up or strive to attain your goals.

We already know that setting worthy goals is how charismatic leaders inspire others, so you cannot let yourself be distracted by negativity.

It's not uncommon for great leaders to feel a range of distracting emotions, but they have strategies in place to cope. They know that if they let themselves be influenced by unwanted feedback, they'd never accomplish anything.

You can think of it as all your emotions—fear, insecurity, joy, envy, love—coexisting under your charisma. Your charisma has to emerge in the eyes of the world as **your most defining quality**. Your other emotions will never disappear, but they will be controlled by your charisma and go barely noticed. This not only means that you will have control of yourself, but also that your presence is felt because it reveals a stronger, more confident version of yourself.

## Diversion Emergence

The process through which you minimize other emotions and **favor charisma** will be known as "**Diversion Emergence**" because you divert all weakening emotions aside leaving your charisma room to grow.

This technique involves focusing on the **opposite of any negative emotion** that is plaguing you. The opposing positive emotion *neutralizes* or *cancels out* the negative emotion.

The best time to do this is first thing in the morning before you get started on your day. When you wake up feeling negative, prepare for your day with the following counting ritual.

You must inhale on <u>one</u> and <u>two</u>, and exhale when you get to <u>three</u>.

*Count 1:* start inhaling,
*Count 2:* finish your intake of air, and
*Count 3:* block the negative thought or feeling by exhaling and directing your mind at a positive thought.

Congratulations! You've just diverted unnecessary emotions!

Again, this should be done as a morning ritual to prepare yourself to not to let anything overwhelm you and to let a stronger, more neutral you emerge through your presence. This will help make an amazing impression on others.

However, in addition to the morning ritual, you can also use it throughout the day, for example, when you are bombarded with too much work and you feel overwhelmed. Instead of letting it ruin your day, divert this feeling by counting 1 and 2 while inhaling, then on 3, blocking the thought or feeling. Just exhale and direct your mind to the opposite.

In this case, since you were feeling **overwhelmed**, the opposite might be **energetic**. You've diverted *overwhelming* somewhere else to let something more motivating like *energetic* take its place and reveal a more appealing you.

Let's use an example to show how versatile this is.

Example: Imagine that the family dog has just passed on. The kids are crying. Maybe you have had this dog for 15 years; you had it even before your kids were born, you have every reason to be affected too, but somebody has to be strong and help the others cope with the situation. However, it can be difficult to offer consolation when you are also feeling grief. Attempts can end up being gruff or cold. Instead of being rough on your family, divert any unnecessary emotions that would not serve anyone well and end up making things worse.

So count:

*Count 1:* start inhaling,

*Count 2:* finish your intake of air, and

*Count 3:* block your grief by exhaling and direct your mind at a positive thought like *hope* or *empathy*

Your negative feelings will melt away and your mind will be free to come up with a comforting message such as, "It was his time to go and he wouldn't want to see us sad." You have diverted sadness and found a way to inspire others with a positive resolution: to accept the situation and move on.

## Divert Other's Negative Feedback

To use "**Diversion Emergence**" to block negative feedback, use the same counting exercise.

Example: Let's say that you have to give a performance or presentation in front of an audience of 100. You are prepared and confident but as usual the anxiety of confronting 100 people can be overwhelming. As you enter the room people are smiling, laughing, and whispering and you start having negative thoughts, losing self-confidence, and feeling doubt. The body language of the crowd makes you think they will enjoy seeing you mess up. At this moment you can divert that thought by counting.

*Count 1:* start inhaling,

*Count 2:* finish your intake of air, and

*Count 3:* block your fear of failure by exhaling and direct your mind at a positive thought like winning

You can also use this technique verbally by blocking unwanted comments from other people with smooth, polite responses.

Going back to that example, which you have now regained your confidence and are about to start your presentation, someone yells "Dude, where did you buy that shirt!" People start laughing.

You need to keep your calm, count to 3, and divert this feedback by saying something like "Is it Fashion Week?" This is straight to the point and people will give you credit because after all you came to make a point and not serve as a fashion model.

The point is to deescalate a situation. It works like a shield that stops unnecessary emotions from destroying your motivation. It prepares you to shine during the day and stops negative feedback from reaching you. You need to take a few seconds every day to practice this technique so you are prepared to let the best of you come out.

## Exercise: <u>Out</u> Emerging Positivity

Try to imagine the following scenarios and find a way to divert negativity mentally or verbally.

Practice breathing and counting to 3 while choosing a positive emotion to divert your energy to.

If you finish these exercises, think of a few of your own scenarios. You can never have too much practice!

1.) You wake up in the morning and there's no more sugar for your morning coffee.

2.) You see a homeless person freezing outside.

3.) Your coworker sneers at you for no reason.

4.) Your family and friends surprise you with a party but you are very tired because of work.

5.) Your 6 year old is very disrespectful to a cashier at the grocery store.

6.) Someone cuts the line in front of you and gives you a threatening look.

*CHAPTER 4*

# Act on the Bright Side of Things as a Charismatic Person

### Inspirational Interaction

We've already gone over focus and presence, now it's time to go over your interactions with others.

Interacting with others plays a huge role in imposing your personality and letting people get to know you. It might be hard to believe, but few interactions are memorable.

However, those few interactions you do have with a highly charismatic person can have a long-lasting impact.

People feel cheered up after speaking to someone with charisma.

> Example: If you were a doctor seeing a patient, you would not only provide a cure, but also speak to the patient and give counseling and recommendations in a very comforting way. When your patient leaves your practice, they already feel good and always remember the feelings they had when they started receiving treatment.

Can you imagine yourself inspiring someone like this? It is hard for a doctor to kind of inspire so many patients day in and day out, but the really good ones do so.

At the same time, charismatic people know how to turn a negative interaction into a positive one. They encounter the same surly and impolite people that we do. The difference is how they react to negativity and how they internalize the interaction.

A truly charismatic person has the ability to put a rude person in their place or win them over with empathy. There are a lot of ways to get people on your side that charismatic people utilize all the time. For them saying the right thing just comes naturally and so they live their lives surrounded by positivity.

## The Charisma Bounce Reminder

The thing you can do to attain a charismatic state whenever you need it is to use the "**Charisma Bounce Reminder**," which acts as mental conditioning where you visualize a **ball of light** filled with positivity bouncing towards the other person and exploding into positivity. This can be represented by whatever mood is suited for the other person, flowers for children, smiley faces for angry coworkers, confetti for your fun-loving friends, etc.

Imagining a physical object like a ball representing your words is a way to make this idea concrete. It's basically *dodgeball* except you are trying to hurl as much positivity around you as possible onto the people. The more positivity you throw, the more will be thrown at you.

Example: You go to work and start interacting with your coworkers. When you greet them or make jokes, see the ball going from you going towards the people you are communicating with and exploding into smiley faces raining down on them. After the visualization process, say something to give them the positivity that you've just visualized.

This becomes a constant visual reminder for you to pull yourself out of whatever state you're in to be positive, cheery, and charismatic with other people, like New Year's Eve when the ball drops where everybody feels a renewed sense of optimism.

Remember that the explosion of positivity can be symbolized by anything such as magical stardust or confetti reminding you of New Year's or some fiestas signifying it's time to be happy and celebrate life.

The imagery of the ball teaches your mind to react faster and to think about the impact your reactions have on those around you. Charismatic people always look for the positive in other people and don't focus on the negative.

Here are examples for different contexts so you can see the types of things this visualization should inspire you to say:

1.) **Conversation with a neighbor**: "Hi! You look lovely today. Looks like someone is being taken care of..."

• This intro will put a smile on their face.

2.) **Conversation with a coworker**: "I am telling you there's nothing like working as hard as we do. One day our kids will take over because we've led the way. Never forget that!"

- This is a simple conversation that is empowering because you remind the other person that you appreciate their hard work.

3.) **Conversation with the grocer**: "Customers come and go but nobody can do what you do. It takes guts to do your job as well as you do."

- This is an example of a warm and caring message that reminds the person that they count and should carry on being such a useful member of the community.

4.) **Interaction with youngsters at the corner**: "Hey! What do you want to be when you grow up?"

- A good example of an inspiring intro to a conversation where these young people feel they have someone to open up to like a big brother or a big sister.

5.) **Interaction with an elderly person**: "The actions you took throughout your life have taught the younger generations well."

- This is a respectful interaction that might bring tears to the eyes of that person.

These examples of wordings during conversations should be inspired by the ball visualization. This ball is a guiding tool telling you, "you must say something inspiring" or "be more charismatic now!"

### Exercise: Preset Positive Interaction

Now practice the following:

1.) Throughout your day, visualize the ball leaving you then exploding positivity onto whoever you're talking to.

2.) After visualizing the ball, start conversing to sound inspiring.

## Deflect Then Respect

We've already talked about using the "Charisma Bounce Reminder" to always see the positive in other people.

Now let's talk about using this to confront negativity around you by taking it another step further with "**Deflect then Respect.**"

Just as you learned to represent positivity using a ball of light, you will now learn to represent negativity with a **ball of water**. With this approach, a negative comment coming at you is like a **water ball** that will splash right in your face.

Negativity should bounce off you, so bounce the water ball off by replying with something positive, represented by your ball of light. When the ball explodes positivity on your audience, they will reply with the same positivity.

This visualization is important because you will notice that if you throw a water ball of negativity, you will have it immediately returned to you. The only way to prevent yourself from being drenched head to toe in negativity is to throw more positivity.

Example: Someone tries to criticize your work as a writer. You've just finished writing your best piece of poetry so far and to get some encouragement, you ask your friend to give you some feedback. Instead of encouraging you they say: "I don't get it. What is this?" If you were to use the "**Charisma Bounce Reminder**" to react, you would do the following:

STEP 1: Process what your friend has just said by visualizing a water ball about to soak you.

<u>STEP 2</u>: Counteract it by making it bounce off you with something positive like "It might not be good but I will get better soon!"

Your positivity will be unexpected, and they will certainly reciprocate. You have bounced the negative off to receive something positive instead. Soaking averted.

If you act positively towards people, positivity will come back to you. It's like karma: you get out of the world exactly what you put into it. Therefore, if you said something positive you will get back something positive in return.

### <u>Exercise</u>: Bouncing Negativity

Now practice the following:

1.) Visualize a negative comment that can affect you like a water ball exploding in your face.

2.) Make it bounce off by saying something positive.

Remember that the principle is to visualize chucking a positivity ball to avoid having negativity splashed all over you. Acting this way will enhance your charisma overnight and encourage you to interact more positively with others.

*CHAPTER 5*

# Support the People Around You as a Charismatic Person

## The Diplomat Who Cares

Diplomacy can be described as negotiation for peace or good relations.

So how does diplomacy equate to being charismatic?

Being diplomatic will not only lead to you knowing how to handle and manage different people, but also appear fair when resolving conflicts. Take for instance relationships: diplomacy takes place every time when we must handle the issues faced with our spouses, friends, colleagues, clients, etc.

When you play the diplomatic role with the people around you, it shows you actually care about them, like creating a protective barrier for the purpose of protection, guidance, and control.

## The Field Of Charisma

This next strategy consists of creating an **imaginary semi-circle** field protecting the people around you with its extremities touching you on your left and right sides.

Each time you create this imaginary field, visualize three words that will guide your mindset like a personal mission: protect, guide, and control. (To clarify, control in this context doesn't mean to manipulate people to bend them to your will. It speaks the positive impact you will have on people.)

How do you protect, guide, and control people? It's simple, use diplomacy. The words are just a reminder to prepare a certain mindset.

Example: Pretend you are a teacher and that during lunch break you are approached by a group of students. As soon as you look at them, visualize a semi-circle field around them and as you visualize the circle, the word "protect" at your bottom left, "guide" in the center, and "control" at your bottom right will start appearing like sparks. This will condition you to be diplomatic no matter what you hear.

# Figure A.*

**CHARISMA THROUGH DIPLOMACY, LIKE A MENTOR OR PARENT**

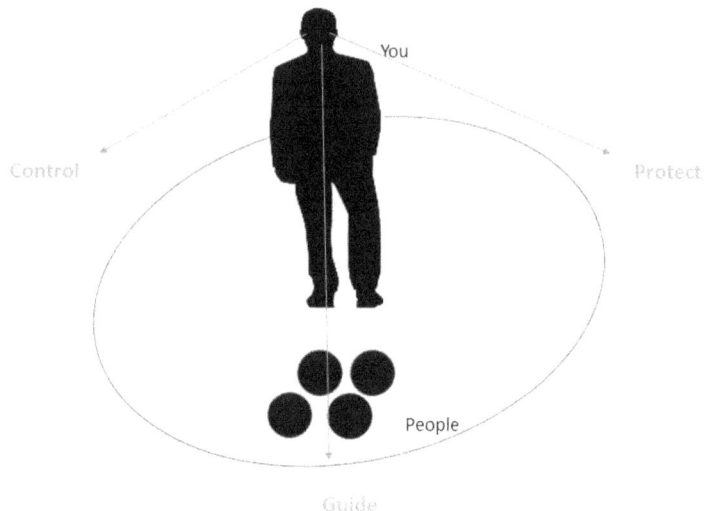

*Figure A. summarizes a diplomatic mindset for charisma. You must imagine a semi-circle field. Visualize the words protect, guide, and control around the circle on the left, center, and right. This will limit you to the role of diplomat. Remember that in this case controlling means gaining recognition or having an impact on people.

## Exercise: Create Charisma Circle

Gather four objects in front of you and practice your field of charisma by doing the following:

Imagine a semi-circle around you and the objects, pretending the objects are people. When you are done with the circle, start visualizing the following words: protect, guide, and control on your left, center, and right, respectively. Get used to this semi-circle field, the three words around you, and the imaginary people.

Next put yourself in the following situation:

1.) Someone wants your advice on how to pick the right career after university.

2.) Write down how you can inspire them with recommendations by being charismatic. Think to yourself, "What can I say that can lead me to protect, guide, and control them?"

## CHAPTER 6

# Perform the Actions as a Charismatic Person

Now that we've covered all the basic techniques for gaining charisma, you need practice! Just as learning a new instrument takes practice, so does crafting a new charismatic lifestyle.

Try each of the exercises below and feel free to add your own ideas. It is important that the circumstances are relatable, so use your imagination to tailor them to you.

### Exercise 1: Hone The Focus

Practice being focused by using the "**Neutrality Lure**" in the following circumstances.

a.) Someone makes an unpleasant remark to you about a young overweight woman.

b.) Your friend asks you if you are mad about them going away for the weekend with someone you like.

Remember to adopt the right gestures like crossing your hands in front of your belly to send the signal to your brain to act naturally (Stand, Signal, Speak).

### Exercise 2: Double Negative Equals Positive

Practice having presence by using the "**Diversion Emergence**" in the following situations:

a.) Your spouse responds in an annoyed tone to your request for help finding the car keys.

b.) Your wake up in the morning feeling unrested, and you don't feel like doing anything.

c.) You're self-conscious about some weight you've put on, and you hear people laughing near you when you're ordering some ice cream.

Remember that you must block negative feedback by diverting it verbally or mentally. Think one, two, take a small breath, three, exhale and replace negativity with positivity, i.e., an insult with a smile.

## <u>Exercise 3</u>: See The Good All Around

Practice seeing the positive in everybody and everything by using the "**Charisma Bounce Reminder**" in the following situations:

a.) You weren't paying attention to directions from your coworker, and he or she calls you out on it.

b.) Your aunt has no kids, and you see her work hard for her nephews and nieces.

c.) You are in a job interview and in the middle of it, the interviewer asks you: "With all your qualifications, why are you still looking for a job at your age?"

## Exercise 4: Protect, Guide, And Control

Create a "Charisma Circle" for the next time you interact with people. Whether they ask for your advice or confide in you, draw an imaginary field:

- What is your advice or argument to them? What type of recognition did you get from them in the end?

*CHAPTER 7*

# Live the Life as a Charismatic Person

The thing about charisma is that it's not about wearing a tailored suit or flying in first class; it's merely the way you act in situations that radiate positivity and reject negativity. It's about empowering yourself and in turn empowering others around you.

These four main areas we have covered—vision, presence, interaction, and diplomacy—will improve your charismatic self. Your mind and imagination will be your best allies as they will help you apply simple but substantial concepts overnight that will lead you to the results you seek.

Remember that charisma is not a one day thing; it's a choice to carry for the rest of your life. A charismatic person is someone who is supposed to inspire others by their actions and decisions. It's not a fantasy. It's real and you must accept that people will want to imitate you or see you as a role model, in the long run.

Now it's time to work on your charismatic lifestyle. Prepare to start witnessing the benefits of your new charisma and be a better version of yourself every day.

Charisma Express

# Now You Know!

We have now gone from - *NOT knowing*...to *KNOWING*.

Doesn't it feel great? As cliché as the proverbial saying goes: knowledge is, indeed, power. The more you know, the more empowered you become. Not knowing is defeating, as you succumb to feelings of helplessness and surrendering of your own self.

Of course, acquiring knowledge is a never-ending quest. There is a great saying by Nobel Prize French author Andre Gide: "Believe those who are seeking the truth. Doubt those who find it."

At the very least, we hope we have set you off in the right path in regards to what you have set out to know, and that you have enjoyed our little journey together for the time you have spent with us.

If you can tell us how we did, that would be very appreciated! We value your feedback and always look forward to hearing from you, or if there is any way we could improve the entire experience for you. If you have a success story, even better - please let us know!

http://www.KnowItExpress.com

Don't forget to stay in contact for we would love to connect with you.

https://www.facebook.com/KnowItExpress
https://twitter.com/KnowItExpress
https://plus.google.com/+KnowItExpress

**What would you like to know? Let us know!**

CONTACT US

Now onward for more power to you, and thank you!

Charisma Express